The Wonder of
PANDAS

For R.J. and Max the dog
— Kathy Feeney

Please visit our web site at: www.garethstevens.com
For a free color catalog describing Gareth Stevens Publishing's list of high-quality books
and multimedia programs, call 1-800-542-2595 (USA) or 1-800-461-9120 (Canada).
Gareth Stevens Publishing's Fax: (414) 332-3567.

Library of Congress Cataloging-in-Publication Data available upon request from publisher.
Fax: (414) 336-0157 for the attention of the Publishing Records Department.

ISBN 0-8368-2768-6

First published in North America in 2001 by
Gareth Stevens Publishing
A World Almanac Education Group Company
330 West Olive Street, Suite 100
Milwaukee, WI 53212 USA

This edition is based on the book *Pandas for Kids,* text © 1997 by Kathy Feeney, with illustrations
by John F. McGee, first published in the United States in 1997 by NorthWord Press, (Creative
Publishing international, Inc.), Minnetonka, MN, and published in a library edition as *Panda Magic
for Kids* by Gareth Stevens, Inc., in 2000. Additional end matter © 2001 by Gareth Stevens, Inc.

Photographs © 1997 by Tom and Pat Leeson. Additional photography © Pan Wenshi/National
Geographic Image Collection, 36-37; Lu Zhi/National Geographic Image Collection, 34-35.

Printed in the United States of America

1 2 3 4 5 6 7 8 9 05 04 03 02 01

The Wonder of
PANDAS

by Patricia Lantier and Kathy Feeney
Illustrations by John F. McGee

Gareth Stevens Publishing
A WORLD ALMANAC EDUCATION GROUP COMPANY

The misty mountains of southwestern China are home to some amazing animals. They are giant pandas. These playful, roly-poly creatures look like big, white balls of fur. Black fur covers their legs and ears and forms a circle around each eye.

Giant pandas are China's national symbol. Long ago, many pandas lived in China's bamboo forests. Now, with only about a thousand wild pandas left, they are very rare.

Giant pandas are an endangered species that might one day become extinct. To protect pandas, China has special areas where they can live safely. Scientists there protect the pandas and take care of them if they are hurt or sick.

China
shares
pandas
with zoos
worldwide,
so more
people will
learn about
these shy
and gentle
animals.

Wild pandas now live only in China, but they once lived in other parts of Asia, such as Vietnam, Laos, and Burma (now called Myanmar).

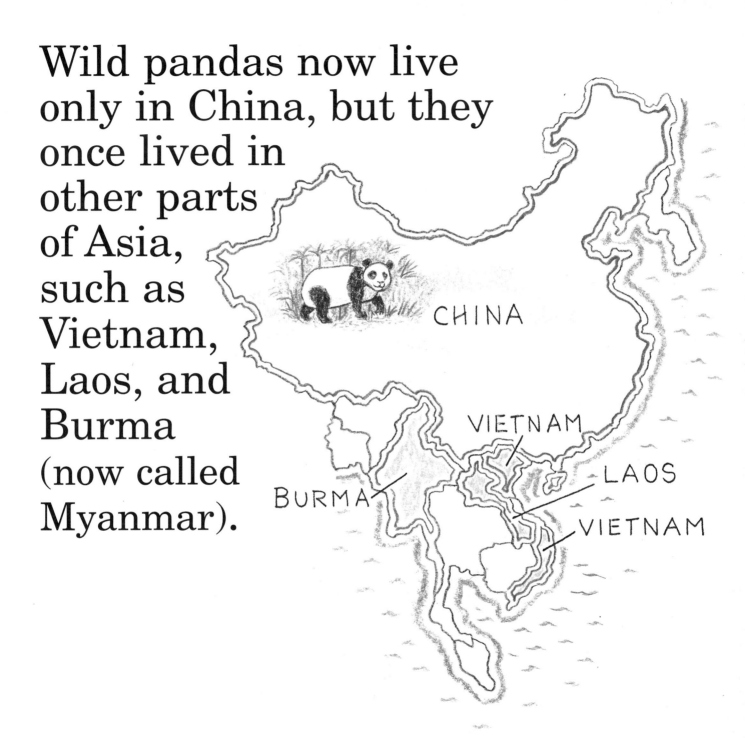

CHINA

VIETNAM

BURMA

LAOS

VIETNAM

Giant pandas are not really giants. It would take about fifty pandas to weigh as much as one elephant.

Although they seem plump and slow, giant pandas are actually very good climbers with amazing balance. They will trot like horses when they are frightened. They can swim, too.

Pandas climb trees when they need a safe place, but they spend most of their time walking. Their fur-padded paws are like snowshoes, so pandas can walk easily, even on snow and ice.

Although pandas look very soft, their fur is stiff and bristly. To clean their fur, they roll in dirt! Then they scrape the dirt out with their claws and wash up by licking their fur.

Pandas have poor eyesight. Sometimes they will walk right past their food and not even see it. Bamboo stalks are a panda's favorite food.

A single panda can eat
about 25,000 pounds
(11,340 kilograms) of
bamboo in one year.
It needs a lot of bamboo
because the stalks are
not very nutritious.
Pandas snack on fruit,
roots, wildflowers, birds,
fish, and eggs. Some even
sneak honey from beehives.

Pandas spend up to fourteen hours a day eating. When they are not eating, pandas sleep. Their naps usually last from two to four hours. Some pandas even snore!

Giant pandas look a lot like bears, but scientists are not sure if pandas are even related to bears. Red pandas look like raccoons and are the size of a large cat.

red panda

Giant pandas have a thumb and five fingers on each front paw. They use their fingers and thumbs to peel the tough, woody bamboo stalks, so they can eat the tender centers.

Pandas are usually quiet creatures. They even leave each other silent messages by clawing on tree trunks.

But pandas can also make sounds to "talk." They bark, bleat, chirp, growl, honk, yip, snort, squeal, and roar.

Baby pandas are called cubs. A mother panda usually has only one or two cubs at a time. Cubs are born in autumn. A newborn panda is so small it can fit into the palm of a person's hand.

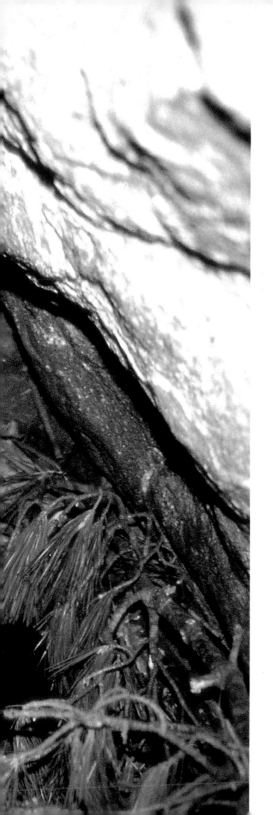

A panda cub drinks
its mother's milk.
It nurses for up
to fourteen hours
a day. When a
mother panda has
to go out to find
food, she holds the
cub close to her
chest with one paw.

Before they are two years old, panda cubs have learned enough to live on their own. A giant panda usually starts a family when it is four years old.   In the wild, pandas can live to be about twenty-five years old.

Full-grown pandas are
about 5 feet (1.5 meters)
long from nose to tail.
Adult pandas weigh
200 to 350 pounds
(90 to 160 kg).

The giant panda is one of the most popular animals in the world. Scientists are working hard to save these threatened animals by studying how pandas live in their habitats. Researchers put special radio collars on them. Then, when the pandas go back into the wild, beeps from the collars send data to the researchers.

Pandas are one of China's national treasures. It is against the law to capture or kill giant pandas. The Chinese government protects them and their habitats so these unique animals can continue to live peacefully in their bamboo forest homes.

47

Glossary

bamboo — a tall, grasslike plant that is found in tropical areas; the stems are woody with hollow centers

bristly — short and coarse, like the bristles of a brush

data — pieces of information, usually used in research

endangered — in danger or peril of dying out completely

extinct — no longer alive

habitats — places where certain animals and plants live in nature

nurse (v) — to drink milk from the body of the mother

nutritious — able to provide nourishment as food or vitamins

researchers — people who carefully study problems or subjects

species — a group of animals or plants with similar characteristics

Index